Welcome & Thank you

Congratulations

Self Care is important and you have taken a step forward by purchasing this workbook. I commend you for understanding how important your well being is. You have made yourself a priority. Doing so not only benefits you, but the people you love as well. The people who love you and depnd on you would much rather see you positive, full of energy and happy, than tired, unhappy and emotionally drainged.

This self care workbook will help to equip you with the knowledge and tools to make self care an ongoing part of your life's journey.

Thank you for choosing our workbook to assist you with your journey

Moreen Jordan, M.A., L.P.C.
Marital & Family Therapist

All rights reserved.
This publication is designed to provide information & enjoyment only.
It is sold with the understanding that the publisher and author is not engaged in rendering psychological, financial, legal or other professional services. Neither the publisher nor the author is engaged in rendering professional services or advice.
For more information contact moreenthetherapist@gmail.com

Copyright @ 2021 by Moreen Jordan, M.A., L.P.C.
www.moreenjordan.com

The ideas, procedures, and suggestions contained in this book are not intended as a substitute for consulting with your physician or other health care provider. All matters regarding your health require medical supervision. Neither the author nor the publisher shall be liable for responsible for any loss or damages allegedly arising from any information or suggestion in this book.
If expert assistance or counseling is needed, the services of a competent professional should be sought.
All handouts and worksheets can be photocopies for personal use with this program, but may not be reproduced for any other purpose without the written permission of the copyright owner.

ISBN: (paperback)
978-1-7373521-7-4

Printed in the United States of American

First Edition 2021
First Printing 2021

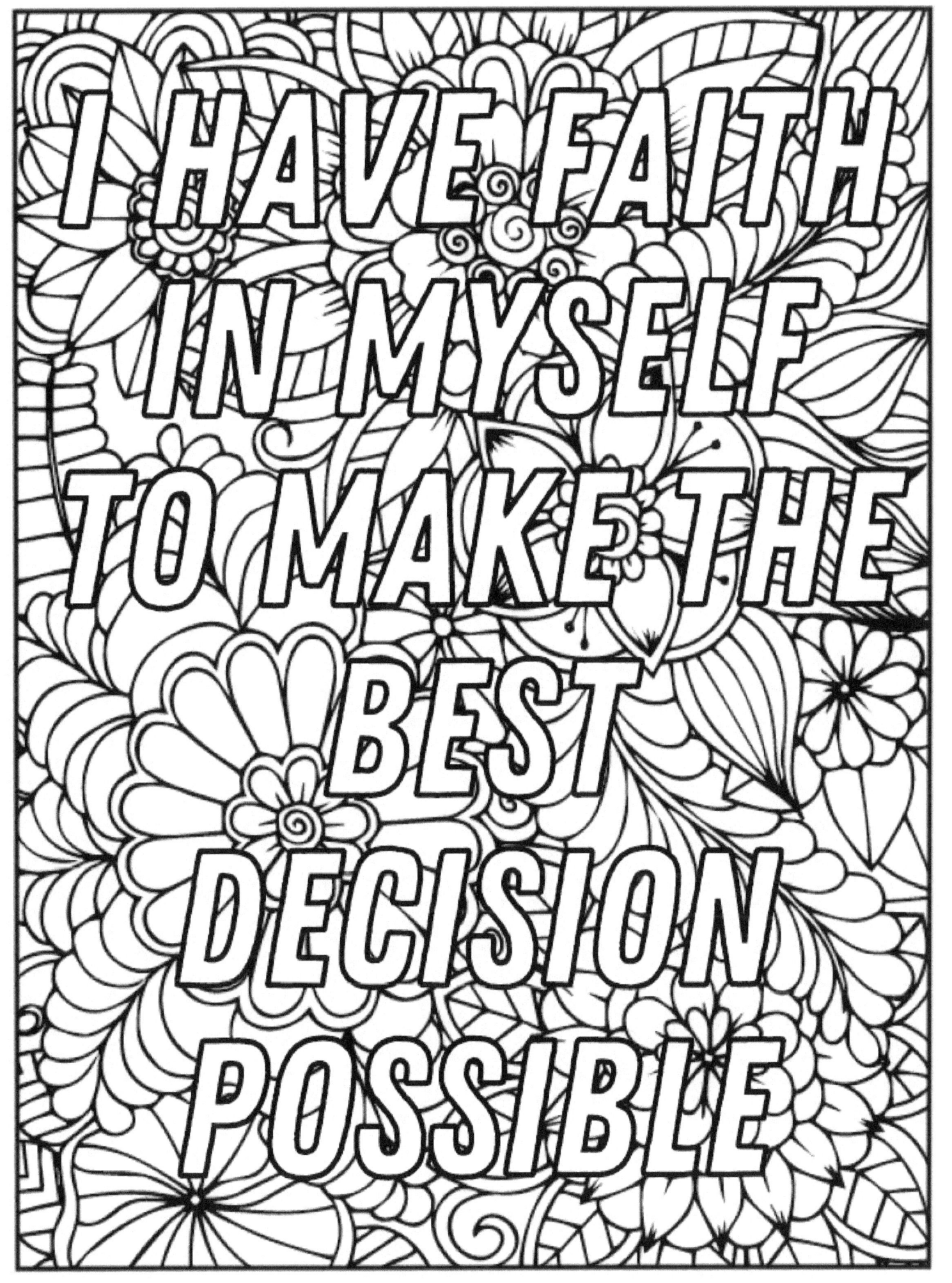

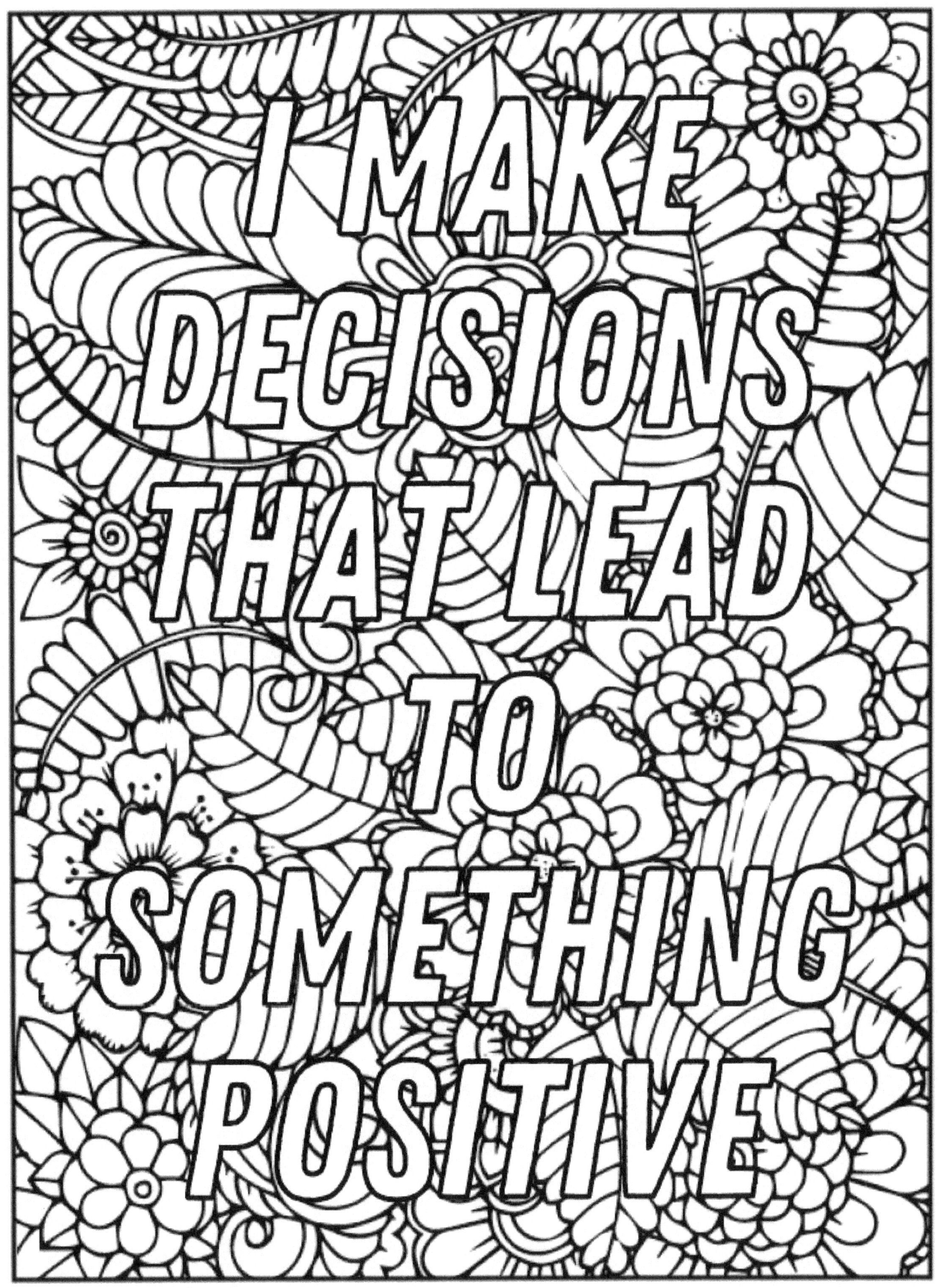

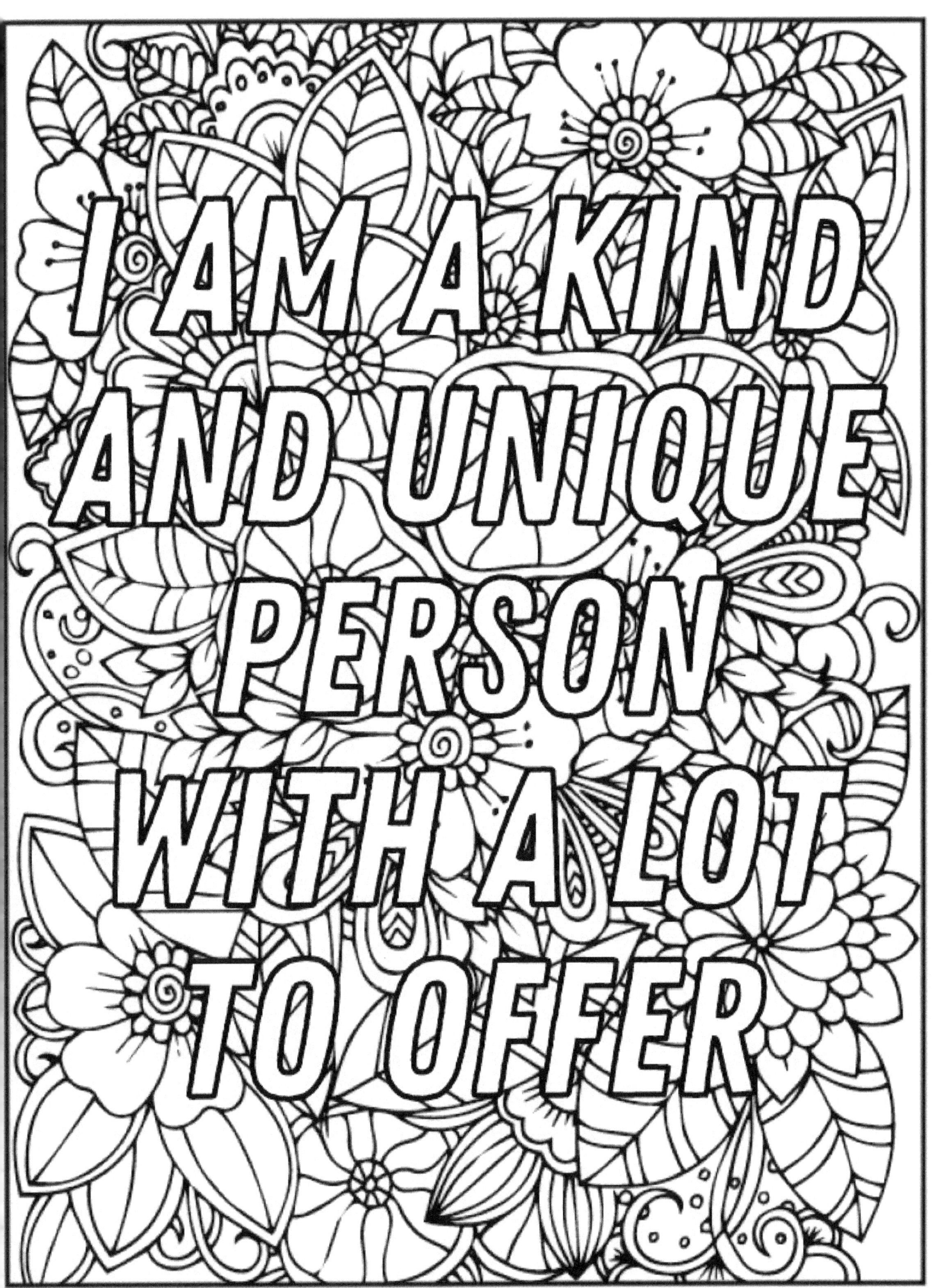

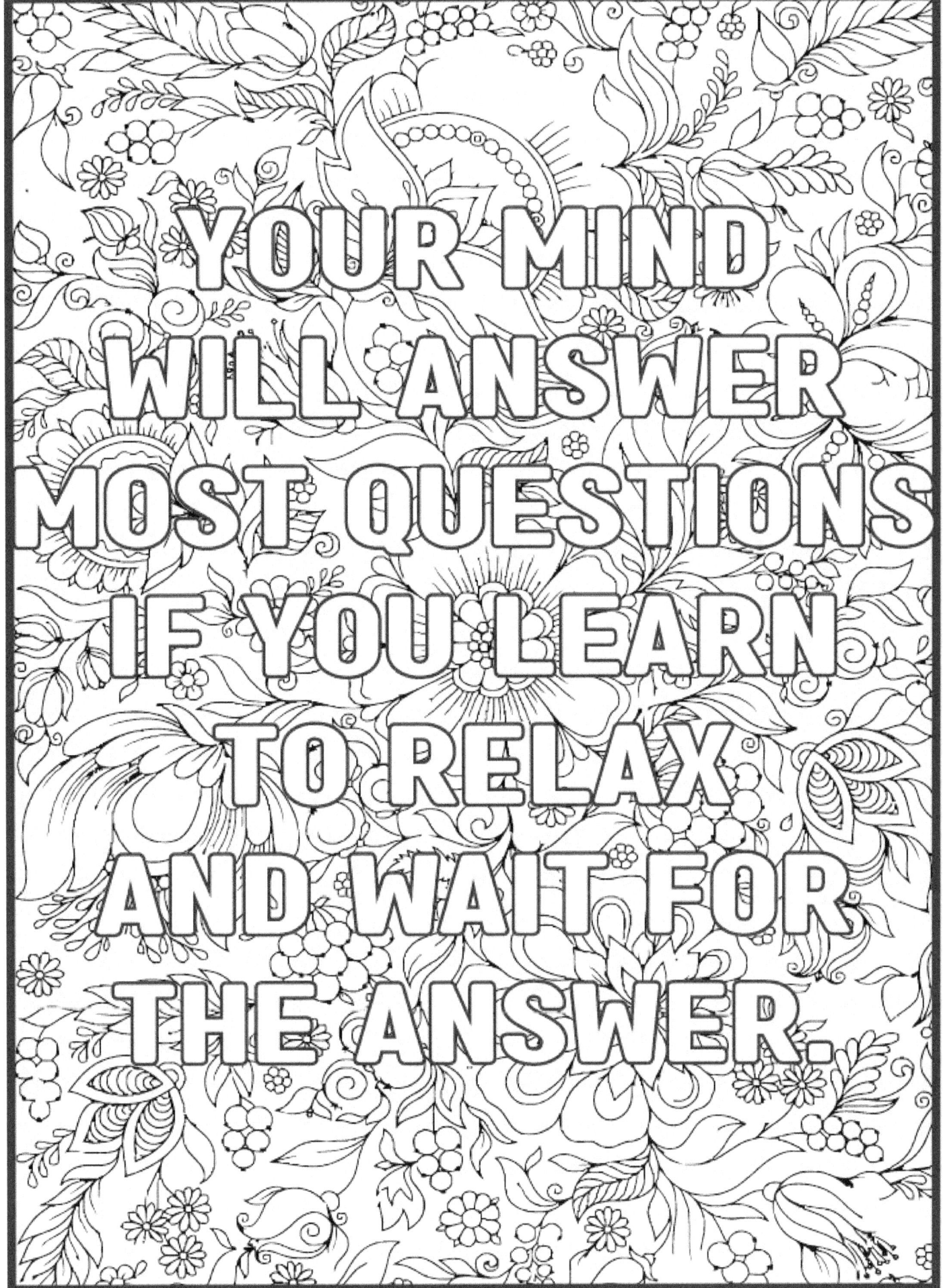

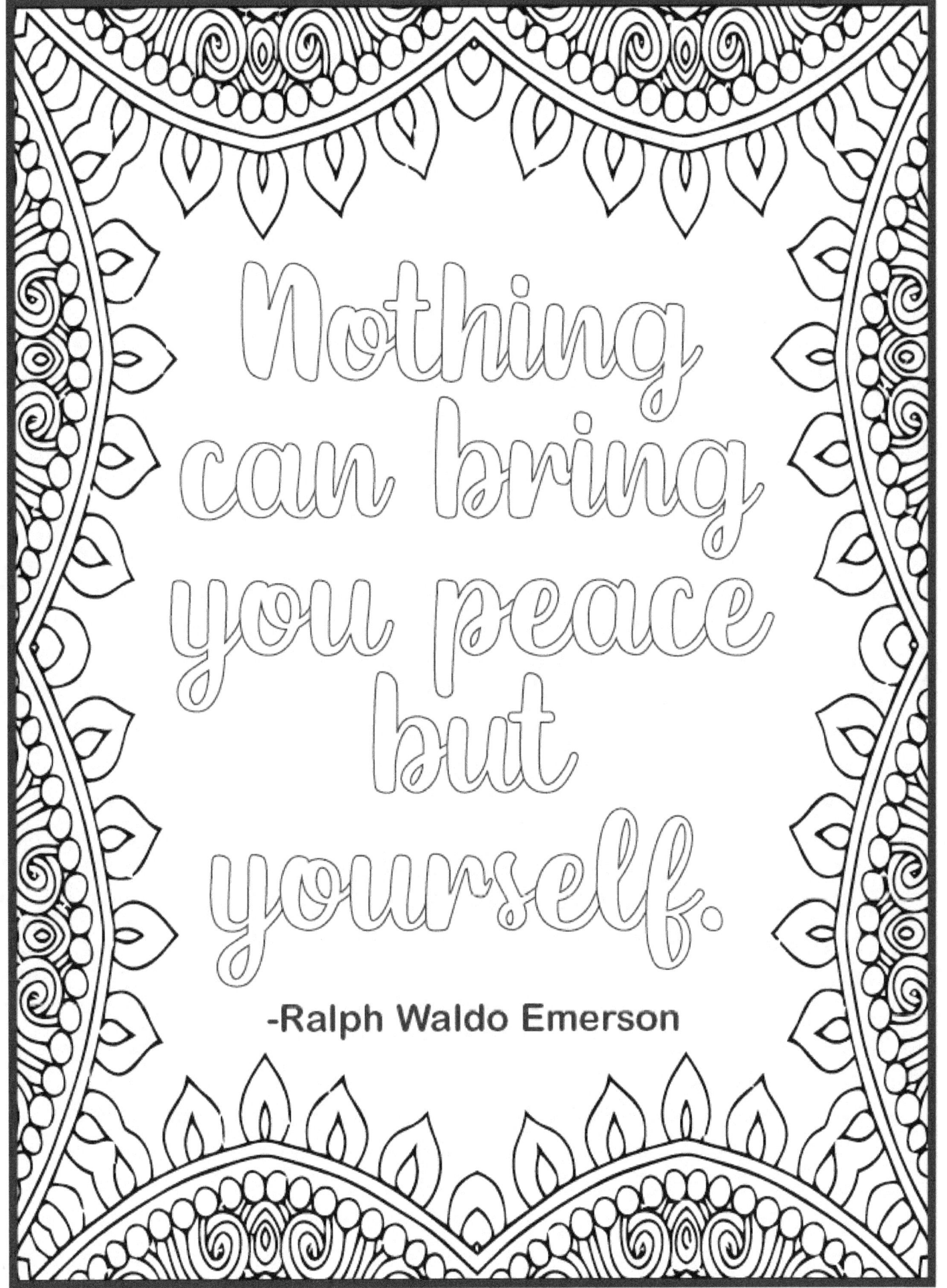

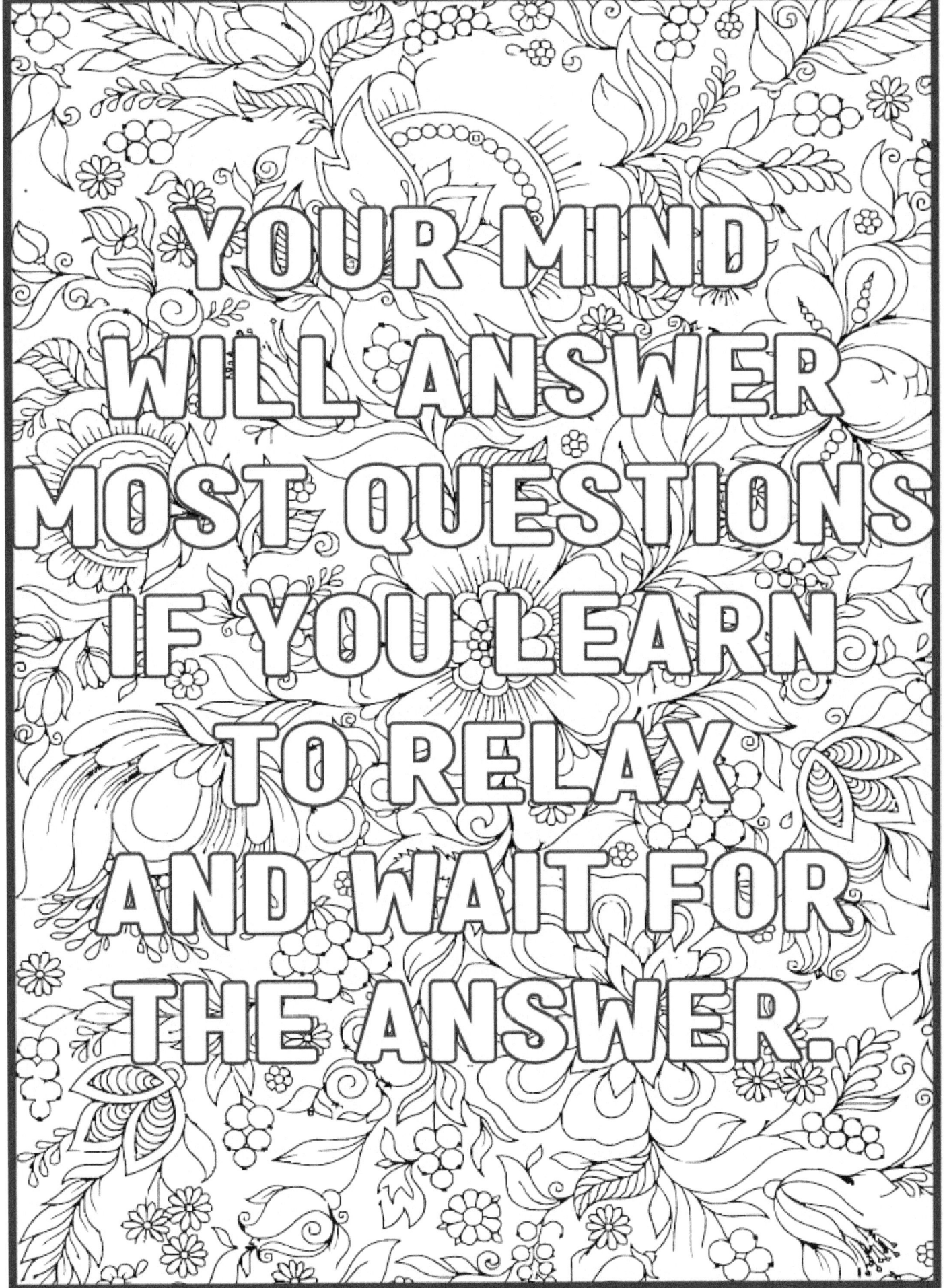

Let's Connect

Newsletter

Sign up for our monthly newsletter and receive up to date information on new products and information to assist and support you in your continued personal growth and so much more.

https://www.moreenjordan.com

and go to sign up for Newsletter

Social Media Facebook:

@ AspiringLifeChange Counseling & Consulting

Website

https://www.moreenjordan.com

Wrapping Up!

Self care is extremely important. You can give more, and you can become more connected with yourself. You will be able to handle stress better and you can become more productive in your day and relationships. These are just a few of the benefits of effective self care. It is important to re-evaluation your self care levels and needs throughout your life. You can take the self care quiz whenever you feel there has been life changes and your need to re-evaluate if you are still addressing caring well for yourself

You can do this.
You deserve this!
Self care is not selfish!

www.ingramcontent.com/pod-product-compliance
Lightning Source LLC
Chambersburg PA
CBHW081419080526
44589CB00016B/2599